Mummies & Pyramids

Sam Taplin

Designed by Stephanie Jones

Illustrated by John Woodcock

Additional illustrations by Ian Jackson

Consultant: Dr. Anne Millard

Series editor: Gillian Doherty

Contents

A chest containing model servants from an Egyptian tomb

Internet links

Look for the Internet links boxes throughout this book. They contain descriptions of Web sites where you can find out more about mummies and pyramids. For links to these Web sites, go to **www.usborne-quicklinks.com** and type the keywords "discovery mummies".

★ Next to some of the pictures in the book you will see a symbol like this. Wherever you see one of these symbols, it means that you can download the picture from the **Usborne Quicklinks Web site**. For more information on using the Internet, and downloading Usborne pictures, see inside the front cover and page 46.

Cover: A statue of the pharaoh Ramesses II
Title page: The pyramids at Giza
Left: The funeral mask of Tutankhamun

Mummies and pyramids......................

Ancient Egypt was a long, narrow country along the River Nile. By 5,000 years ago, the Egyptians had created one of the world's first great civilizations. But they are particularly famous for two reasons: they preserved dead people as mummies, and they built huge pyramids as tombs.

What is a mummy?

A mummy is a preserved dead body. Normally, the body of a person or animal starts to decay soon after death, but mummies don't rot like this. Mummification (making mummies) was very important to the ancient Egyptians. They believed that dead people continued living in another world, and they thought that the spirit needed the body in order to enjoy the next world.

As well as people, the Egyptians also made dead animals into mummies. This is the mummy of a calf.

This photograph shows the famous pyramids at Giza, in Egypt.

Internet links

For a link to a Web site where you can find out more about everyday life for rich people and poor people in ancient Egypt, go to **www.usborne-quicklinks.com**

Why "mummies"?

People once thought that the Egyptians used a sticky, black substance called bitumen to preserve their dead. The Arabic word for bitumen is *mummiya*, and from this we get the word "mummy".

Pyramid tombs

The pyramids were built as tombs for the mummies of some Egyptian kings, or pharaohs. No one had ever made such enormous buildings before, and the Great Pyramid at Giza became one of the legendary wonders of the ancient world.

Fact: The Great Pyramid at Giza contains more than two million massively heavy blocks of stone.

Egypt

This map shows where Egypt is in the world.

Studying the past

Pyramids and mummies can tell us a lot about life in ancient Egypt. Studying a mummy can help us to understand what illnesses people suffered from, where they came from and what they ate. The pyramids provide information too. They give us an insight into the building skills and religious beliefs of the Egyptians.

This is the mummy of Petamenophis, an Egyptian official who died about 2,500 years ago.

The afterlife

The Egyptians believed in an afterlife. This means a world beyond this one where people go when they die. Being made into a mummy and buried in a tomb wasn't the end of life, but the start of the greatest adventure of all.

The Field of Reeds

The Egyptians imagined a heaven ruled by a god called Osiris. The kingdom of Osiris was a beautiful sunny land called the Field of Reeds. There, surrounded by golden wheat and fruit trees, people ate, drank and were happy all day long.

The crops in the Field of Reeds were huge, but harvesting them was always easy.   ★

A terrifying journey

Reaching the kingdom of Osiris wasn't easy. First, you had to survive a long and dangerous journey through the murky passages of the Underworld. Blocking your path were evil spirits, deadly snakes and lakes of fire.

A ferryman took you across the River of Death.

Fire-breathing snakes   ★
guarded the way.

This tomb painting shows Osiris, ruler of the Underworld.

Magic charms like this heart amulet were buried with mummies, to help people survive the Underworld.

Weighing the heart

The greatest test came at the end. Your heart was weighed against a feather, and your life was judged by Osiris. If your heart was heavy with wickedness, it would be gobbled up by a monster. But people who had lived a good life could enter the Field of Reeds.

The Book of the Dead

While they were alive, Egyptians learned magic spells to help them face the perils of the Underworld. About 3,500 years ago, these spells were collected and written down in a book known as the Book of the Dead. Wealthy people were buried with a copy of this book, hoping that the spells inside it would protect them on their journey through the Underworld.

This scene from the Book of the Dead shows a person's heart being weighed.

Anubis, god of embalming, held the dead person's hand.

Ammit the 'devourer', who ate the hearts of wicked people

Osiris sat on his throne and judged the dead person.

Internet links

For a link to a Web site where you can use magic spells to defend yourself as you take a journey through the Egyptian Underworld, go to **www.usborne-quicklinks.com**

The royal afterlife

The powerful pharaohs were the only ones who had a different afterlife. Instead of going to the Field of Reeds, they became gods and floated up to join the other gods in the sky.

 Fact: The Egyptians had hundreds of gods and goddesses, who looked after everything from baking bread to fighting battles.

Making mummies

The ancient Egyptians were the most skilled and dedicated mummy-makers in history. Preserving the dead was important to their culture, and they invented a complicated way of doing it.

Canopic jars, decorated with the heads of gods, were used to store the mummy's internal organs. The jars were buried inside the mummy's tomb.

Internet links

For a link to a Web site where you can click on different parts of a mummy to find out more about how mummies were made, go to **www.usborne-quicklinks.com**

Although they are thin and dried out, many mummies are still very well preserved beneath the bandages. This is the pharaoh Ramesses II.

A grisly job

It took the Egyptians 70 days to mummify, or embalm, a body, and the embalmers had to cope with blood, guts and awful smells. First, they pushed a sharp rod up through the nose and into the brain. The brain was broken up and pulled out through the nose.

A hole was made in the body, and the embalmers pulled out all the internal organs except for the heart.

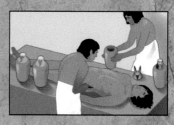

The hole was stuffed with linen and spices, then the body was left under a salt called natron to dry it out.

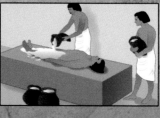

After 40 days, the body was carefully wrapped in linen bandages. Priests said spells while the body was wrapped.

Magnificent masks

When the mummy was finished, a mask was placed over the bandaged face, so that the person could be recognized in the afterlife. Some masks showed a highly realistic portrait of the dead person.

The mummy industry

Lots of people were needed to prepare and bury mummies. There were coffin-makers and tomb-builders, and some people worked as professional mourners. They wailed and screamed at funerals, to show how much the dead person was missed.

This mask was made for a rich woman who died about 2,500 years ago.

Coffins and cases

When the Egyptians had finished making a mummy, they placed it in a coffin to give it extra protection. The earliest coffins were simple cases made from reeds or wood, but later ones were beautifully decorated.

Internet links

For a link to a Web site with a clickable coffin which you can use to find out the meaning behind the paintings on Egyptian coffins, go to **www.usborne-quicklinks.com**

Decorated coffins

About 4,000 years ago, the Egyptians started painting coffins with pictures of objects the dead person might need in the afterlife. The inside was just as carefully decorated as the outside.

Nests of coffins

Early coffins were a simple rectangular shape, but later ones were shaped like people. The mummies of royals and wealthy Egyptians were given special protection by being placed in a nest of two or three human-shaped coffins, one inside the other. The coffins of a pharaoh might be solid gold or silver.

Here you can see the lavishly decorated inside of a human-shaped coffin.

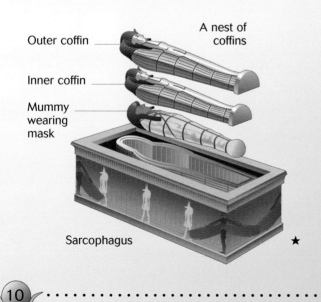

Outer coffin

Inner coffin

Mummy wearing mask

A nest of coffins

Sarcophagus ★

Sealed in stone

The outermost coffin of a pharaoh was a big stone box called a sarcophagus. About 4,500 years ago, these heavy rectangular boxes were left undecorated, or were carved with a picture of a royal palace.

Later, they were carved with pictures of four goddesses, one guarding each corner. By 2,500 years ago, a completely different human-shaped sarcophagus had become fashionable.

This beautifully carved sarcophagus was made for Sasobek, an Egyptian minister who died around 2,500 years ago.

From around 1,300 years ago, a portrait of the dead person was left in their coffin. This portrait shows a wealthy woman wearing earrings and a necklace.

Funerals and grave goods

Once an Egyptian mummy was inside its coffin, it was taken to its tomb in a solemn funeral procession. Then, it was buried along with many objects, known as grave goods. These were meant to help the dead person in the afterlife.

Internet links

For a link to a Web site where you can see photographs of Egyptian grave goods including furniture, model servants and gold treasures, go to www.usborne-quicklinks.com

Journey to the tomb

The coffin was placed on a wooden boat, which was pulled along on a sled by oxen and men. Priests walked ahead, saying prayers and burning sweet-smelling incense. Servants followed, carrying the grave goods for the tomb, while mourners wailed in distress. Later, there was a feast for family and friends, and offerings were made to the dead person's spirit.

★ This glass perfume-holder was buried in an Egyptian tomb.

★

Servants carrying grave goods

The coffin on the funeral boat

Priest spreading incense

Mourners weeping and screaming

This scene shows part of a funeral procession.

Ready for the afterlife

Dead people were expected to continue leading a normal life. So they were buried with an amazing variety of different objects to keep them comfortable and entertained. There were beds, clothes, musical instruments, and even board games.

Wealthy Egyptians were buried with lots of precious jewels and ornaments, such as this golden earring.

Servants and feasts

Dead people were provided with small model servants to look after them, prepare food, keep animals and grow crops in the next world. In later times, people were buried with 365 servants, one for each day of the year.

Real food, such as fruit and meat, was left in the tomb as well. Relatives were supposed to leave more food for the dead person every day, but people mainly did this on important festivals.

The Opening of the Mouth

Before the mummy was sealed inside its burial chamber, a priest performed a ritual known as the Opening of the Mouth. He touched the mummy's ears, eyes and mouth with sacred objects. This was to allow the dead person to hear, see and speak in the next world.

This model servant from an Egyptian tomb is bringing bread for the dead person.

This scene shows priests performing the Opening of the Mouth ceremony.

Houses of eternity.....

Early Egyptians buried people in holes in the desert, and poor people were buried in this way throughout Egyptian civilization. But pharaohs and nobles were laid to rest in tombs that would last forever and show the world their glory.

Internet links

For a link to a Web site where you can see great photos of the first step pyramid and find out more about how it was built, go to **www.usborne-quicklinks.com**

Mastabas

The first royal tombs were called mastabas. These were low, rectangular mud-brick buildings, with a burial chamber built beneath them.

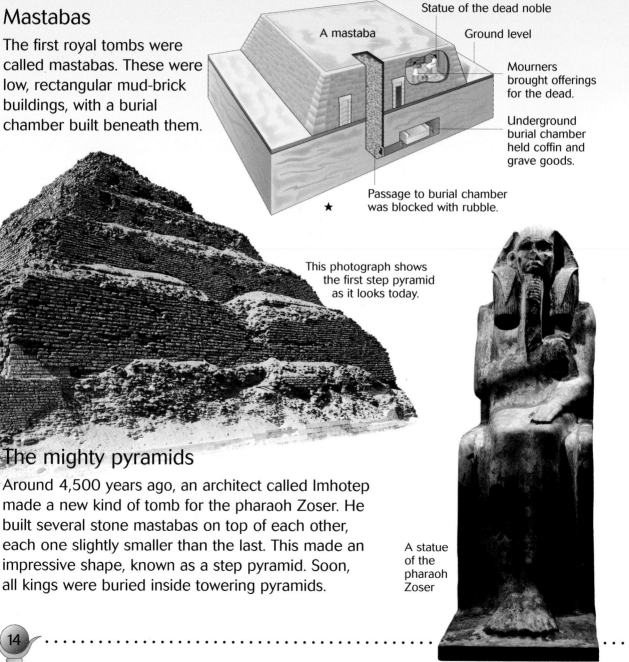

Statue of the dead noble

A mastaba

Ground level

Mourners brought offerings for the dead.

Underground burial chamber held coffin and grave goods.

Passage to burial chamber was blocked with rubble.

This photograph shows the first step pyramid as it looks today.

The mighty pyramids

Around 4,500 years ago, an architect called Imhotep made a new kind of tomb for the pharaoh Zoser. He built several stone mastabas on top of each other, each one slightly smaller than the last. This made an impressive shape, known as a step pyramid. Soon, all kings were buried inside towering pyramids.

A statue of the pharaoh Zoser

This is part of the rock-cut tomb of Nefertari, wife of the pharaoh Ramesses II. Rock-cut tombs were lavishly painted on the inside.

Royal tombs were decorated with paintings of the gods. This is Re-Harakhti, the sun god.

The Valley of the Kings

Pyramids were so spectacular that robbers couldn't resist breaking in and stealing the treasures. About 3,500 years ago, a cunning pharaoh called Tuthmosis I came up with a solution. His tomb was cut deep into the rock of a hidden valley, now known as the Valley of the Kings. This idea caught on, and soon all pharaohs and their wives were buried in secret rock-cut tombs.

Persistent pyramids

Although pharaohs were no longer buried in pyramids, the pyramid shape remained very important to the Egyptians. Some people had miniature pyramids built over their tombs.

Pyramids also made a comeback in the Kingdom of Kush, a part of Egypt which became independent about 2,700 years ago. The people of Kush copied the Egyptian way of life, and the kings built pyramids which are still standing today.

Fact: The Valley of the Kings was said to be protected from robbers by a serpent goddess called Meretseger.

The pyramid builders

The pyramids were miracles of architecture and organization. Without cranes, drills or machines of any kind, the Egyptians created some of the largest stone buildings ever made.

Internet links

For a link to a Web site where you can take a guided photo tour around the outside and inside of the Bent Pyramid, go to **www.usborne-quicklinks.com**

Early experiments

When the Egyptians first tried to make a pyramid with straight sides instead of steps, they made the sides too steep. They tried to correct this by making them less steep at the top, but this left the pyramid looking a little strange. It became known as the Bent Pyramid.

This photograph shows the Bent Pyramid as it looks today.

A massive task

After that, the Egyptians became masters at building pyramids. For 800 years, these towering tombs sprung up in Egypt. They were built with sheer muscle power and dedication, and making a large one might require as many as 20,000 workmen.

The pyramid still has traces of the white stone that once covered the whole building.

Stage by stage

Building a pyramid was an incredibly complicated job, and the work was done slowly and carefully, in many different stages. For the biggest pyramids, the whole process could take over 20 years to complete. A great deal of work had to be done before the first stone block could be set in place.

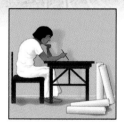

An architect made plans and built models to show to the pharaoh.

Large blocks of stone were carved from quarries with mallets and chisels.

 Fact: About ninety pyramids were built throughout Egypt, and most of these are still standing.

Willing workers

People used to think the pyramids were built by slaves who were treated harshly, but the workers were actually free men. They were paid by the pharaoh, and they were proud to be part of such an amazing achievement.

As well as the builders, a massive number of other people were needed to provide all the stone, feed the workers and transport the blocks from the quarry to the building site. This was such a huge effort of organization that building the pyramids helped to transform Egypt into a powerful and efficient country.

Ancient Egyptian tools were very basic compared to modern ones. Most of them were made of wood, with blades made of stone or soft metal, like copper.

Workmen dragged the blocks to boats, which took them down the river to the pyramid site.

All the sand was removed from the site, and the rock was flattened so it would support the building.

As the pyramid grew, the workmen hauled the blocks up huge ramps studded with wooden rollers.

The ramps were gradually removed, and a layer of gleaming polished stone was added.

★

An adze like this was used for shaping the wooden rollers on the pyramid ramps.

Stone balls like this were used to shape hard rocks.

Chisels were useful for delicately shaping wood.

Mallets and chisels were used to carve and shape stone blocks from the quarry.

Pyramid power

The pyramids were far more than just spectacular buildings. They were deeply influenced by Egyptian religion, and were designed to send the dead king to join his fellow gods in heaven.

An Egyptian star chart showing each constellation in the shape of a god or an animal

Stepladders to the stars

The pyramids had many different meanings for the Egyptians. Early kings believed they would join particular constellations (groups of stars) in the afterlife. Texts written on later pyramids describe step pyramids as stepladders to the stars.

Inside the burial chamber of the Great Pyramid at Giza are two narrow vents pointing upward through the rock. These seem to point directly at constellations that were important in Egyptian religion. The vents may have been intended to launch the pharaoh's soul up to the gods.

Sunbeams made of stone

By about 2,500 years ago, the sun god Re had become very important. Pyramids were now thought of as huge ramps, or sunbeams made of stone. The dead king's soul would climb up these ramps and meet Re in the sky.

This picture shows Re, the sun god, making his daily journey across the sky.

Here you can see the pyramids at Giza, the biggest and most famous in Egypt.

Fact: Temples were built on the eastern side of the pyramids, because this was the direction of the rising sun and rebirth.

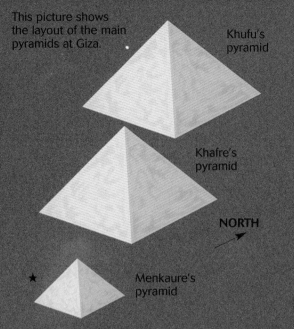

This picture shows the layout of the main pyramids at Giza.

Khufu's pyramid

Khafre's pyramid

NORTH

Menkaure's pyramid

The Giza pyramids are lined up so that their four sides face north, south, east and west. Experts think that the builders used the stars to position them so precisely.

Internet links

For a link to a Web site where you can crawl through the mysterious passageways deep inside the Great Pyramid, go to
www.usborne-quicklinks.com

The city of the dead

Today, we think of the pyramids standing alone in the empty desert, but things were very different in ancient times. Next to each pyramid was a temple where priests presented offerings to the dead king every day.

There were also smaller pyramids where queens were buried and mastaba tombs for members of the king's court. The whole group of buildings was called the necropolis, or the city of the dead.

Nearby were palaces and towns where priests and their families lived. These people spent their lives looking after the pyramids and the dead kings.

Out of the waters

The pyramid shape was also connected with an Egyptian belief about the creation of the world. In the beginning, the world was just water, until a mound of earth rose from the depths. Some people thought of the pyramid as a symbol of this mound.

This small bronze statue shows an Egyptian priest. Priests were powerful in ancient Egypt, and were seen as the servants of the gods.

Tomb raiders

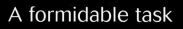

Since many Egyptian mummies were buried with fabulous treasures, cemeteries had to be extremely well guarded. But in chaotic periods when the guards were often away, robbers moved in. If caught they faced an awful death, but many still risked their lives to get hold of the pharaohs' riches.

A formidable task

Breaking into a royal rock-cut tomb was far from easy. The doors were sealed shut with stones, then covered with a layer of plaster. The entrance passages were often blocked with huge stone slabs or filled with rubble, so the robbers had to tunnel through to the tomb.

This is part of the tomb of the pharaoh Ramesses IV. Like almost everything else in the Valley of the Kings, his sarcophagus was robbed thousands of years ago.

The robbers made a small tunnel into a tomb, so that they could cover it up afterwards.

They smashed open the chests of treasures and filled their baskets with gold and jewels.

★

Under cover of night, they loaded their baskets of loot onto donkeys and quickly escaped.

 Fact: Some robbers used stolen treasures as part of the grave goods for their own tombs.

• • • •

Smooth criminals

By about 3,000 years ago, tomb robbing had become a highly organized business. Gangs of raiders had donkeys and boats standing by so they could make a quick getaway. They also prepared secret places to hide all their stolen treasure. Sometimes, tomb guards were paid bribes to keep them quiet.

Modern day robbers

The raiding didn't end with the ancient world. Throughout the centuries, and up to the present day, thieves have continued searching for new tombs to raid. Although tomb robbing is illegal in Egypt, some people are still tempted by the treasures of their ancestors.

Precious objects like this gold necklace have tempted robbers since ancient times.

Magical amulets were left with mummies to protect them, but they didn't discourage robbers.

This statue at Giza is called the Sphinx. A form of the Egyptian sun god, the Sphinx was intended to act as a guardian of the nearby pyramids.

Mummy mania....................................

This is the body of Jeremy Bentham, an English philosopher who asked to be mummified when he died.

The head of Bentham's "mummy" is a wax copy, but his real body is preserved beneath his suit.

In the early 1800s, explorers began bringing back Egyptian mummies and tomb treasures to Europe and America. This created a wave of public interest in the ancient Egyptians, and people were gripped by mummy mania.

Mummy hunters

Soon, Egypt was swarming with wealthy collectors who wanted to find their own mummies. Some of these mummy hunters were serious archaeologists who gave their finds to museums, but others just wanted souvenirs to take home.

Public unwrappings

When collectors returned from their travels, they were eager to show off their discoveries. People were fascinated, and mummy viewings became very popular. Some collectors went even further, and actually unwrapped a mummy before specially invited guests. This wasn't always easy, and on one occasion the mummy had to be sawn open.

A 19th-century drawing of a mummy being unwrapped

 Fact: Not everyone treasured mummies. Some were even used as fuel in steam engines.

Becoming mummies

Some wealthy people got so carried away that they decided to be made into mummies themselves when they died. Other people asked to be buried with Egyptian-style pyramids and obelisks as gravestones.

This is the Washington Monument in the USA, which was built in the shape of an Egyptian obelisk.

Egyptian styles

During the 1920s, when Tutankhamun's tomb was discovered, the interest in ancient Egypt created a new craze for Egyptian-style furniture, buildings and jewels. For a while, a brooch in the shape of an Egyptian scarab beetle was the height of fashion. Even today, Egyptian style has a powerful influence over designers.

A brooch made in the 1930s, shaped to look like the head of an ancient Egyptian pharaoh

Egyptian architecture remains very popular today. These statues are part of a hotel in Las Vegas, USA.

23

The tomb of Tutankhamun........

The most famous Egyptian tomb of all was built for Tutankhamun, the boy king who died when he was not much more than 18 years old.

An early death

Tutankhamun became pharaoh of Egypt around 3,370 years ago, when he was about nine years old. Less than ten years later he was dead, and no one is sure why. Some people have even suggested that he may have been murdered. The young pharaoh was mummified and sealed in a tomb in the Valley of the Kings.

In search of history

Over 3,000 years passed. Most Egyptian royal tombs were ransacked by robbers, leaving only fragments of the treasures which had been buried with the pharaohs. Many experts thought there was nothing left to find. But a few determined archaeologists continued to explore the Valley of the Kings, still dreaming of a discovery.

This wooden portrait bust of Tutankhamun was discovered in his tomb.

Internet links

For a link to a Web site where you can read an exciting account of the discovery of the tomb written by a journalist in 1923, go to **www.usborne-quicklinks.com**

This bracelet from the tomb has a carved scarab beetle, an Egyptian symbol of the sun.

"Wonderful things"

With his sponsor, Lord Carnarvon, by his side, Carter removed a stone from the tomb door. By the light of a flickering candle, he peered into the darkness. When asked if he could see anything, he replied, "Yes, wonderful things!"

The chamber was packed with a dazzling array of statues, chariots, caskets and vases. Gold gleamed everywhere in the candlelight. It was some of the most amazing treasure ever found.

This photograph shows Howard Carter and his assistants opening a shrine inside the tomb.

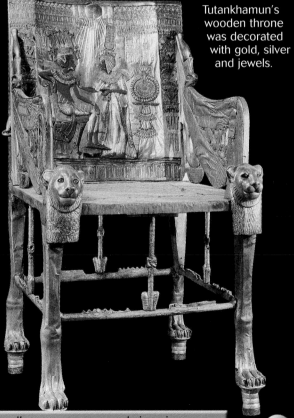

Tutankhamun's wooden throne was decorated with gold, silver and jewels.

An amazing find

In 1922, a British archaeologist named Howard Carter was searching the Valley of the Kings. He had almost given up hope of finding anything new, when beneath the rubble from another tomb he found steps leading down into the rock. He followed them, and eventually came to a plastered wall bearing the seals of Egyptian priests. It was the tomb of Tutankhamun.

Fact: Tutankhamun's tomb was a very small one, so we can only imagine the treasures that once lay in the larger tombs in the Valley of the Kings.

Tutankhamun fever

The discovery of Tutankhamun's tomb thrilled the world. As Carter and Carnarvon removed the treasures, they were surrounded by fascinated onlookers. Hundreds of journalists, photographers and other visitors from across the world flocked to Egypt, hoping for a glimpse of the wonders.

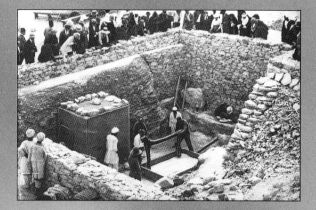

This photograph shows the crowds around the tomb entrance as treasures were removed.

Treasure hoard

Among the objects filling the tomb were statues of gods, painted chests, board games, lamps and necklaces. There was also lots of real food that had been left for the pharaoh. Because there were so many fragile treasures, it took years to remove them all.

This hawk-shaped pendant was just one of the many treasures found in the tomb.

Internet links

For a link to a Web site where you can see lots of photographs of the spectacular treasures found in Tutankhamun's tomb, go to **www.usborne-quicklinks.com**

The moment of truth

Carter soon realized that ancient thieves had broken into the tomb and escaped with a few small items. But no one knew whether the pharaoh's burial chamber, which would contain the most precious treasures of all, had been raided. At last, three years after finding the tomb, Carter was ready to find out.

Meeting the mummy

Inside the burial chamber was a magnificent sarcophagus made of red stone. Within it was a nest of three coffins, the last one made of solid gold. When Carter opened this, he became the first person to see Tutankhamun's mummy in 3,000 years.

Tutankhamun's mummified head

A stunningly beautiful golden mask lay over the face, and more than a hundred amulets and jewels were wrapped up in the bandages. But, sadly, the materials that should have preserved the body had actually damaged it badly.

The golden funeral mask shows a portrait of the young pharaoh.

Beastly bodies

The Egyptians didn't stop at mummifying people. Animals were very important to their religion, and they made them into mummies too.

Sacred beasts

The Egyptians mummified lots of different animals, including cats, crocodiles and baboons. They believed that gods could send their spirit to Earth to enter the bodies of a few special creatures, so it was important to preserve them. For example, Amun, the king of the gods, could appear as a ram or a goose, while a falcon flying overhead might actually be Horus, the sun god.

This is the wall of an Egyptian temple. The ram's head in the middle is a symbol of the god Amun.

Lives of luxury

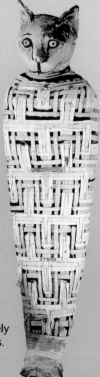

Animals who were thought to represent gods lived next to the god's temple, and were lovingly cared for. When they died, they were made into mummies and buried with a respectful ceremony. Their coffins were sometimes just as beautifully decorated as human coffins.

This golden coffin was made for an ibis, a sacred Egyptian bird.

Some animals, such as this cat, were wrapped in intricately patterned bandages.

A crocodile mummy

Internet links

For a link to a Web site where you can find out more about different types of animal mummies and how they were made, go to **www.usborne-quicklinks.com**

The Apis bulls

Although many animals were made into mummies, a few were particularly important. The most famous is the Apis bull, who was thought to contain the spirit of the god Ptah.

The Apis bull was always black with white markings.

★

The bull was visited by the worshippers of Ptah, and it was thought that it had the power to predict the future. When it died, it was made into a mummy and buried in a huge stone sarcophagus. Then, a new bull was chosen to be the Apis bull.

Dogs were popular pets in ancient Egypt, and lots of them were mummified.

A huge industry

By about 2,500 years ago, Egyptians thought that every single animal contained part of a god's spirit. Making animal mummies became more and more popular, and thousands of people were employed to do the work. People bought these mummies, then buried them in animal cemeteries, as a way of pleasing the gods. Many millions of animals were mummified in this way.

Fact: In the 19th century, thousands of ancient mummified cats were shipped from Egypt to England, to be ground up and used as fertilizer.

29

Myths and movies......................................

Mummies and pyramids have always inspired the imagination. Movies about mummies that come to life are very popular, and people enjoy wild stories about magical powers and curses from beyond the grave.

Internet links

For a link to a Web site where you can read the facts about the mysterious "curse" of Tutankhamun and its victims, go to **www.usborne-quicklinks.com**

The curse of Tutankhamun

Lord Carnarvon (on the left) outside the tomb

The most famous myth of all is the curse said to haunt those who disturbed the mummy of the pharaoh Tutankhamun. Lord Carnarvon, who organized the expedition, died less than a year after entering the tomb. At the moment of his death in Cairo, all the lights in the city went out. At the same time, back in England, his beloved dog howled and died. Other people who were said to have visited the tomb also died.

This is one of two life-size statues that guarded Tutankhamun's burial chamber.

A total invention

Actually, all of these spine-chilling tales are completely untrue. There is no curse written on the wall of Tutankhamun's tomb, and Lord Carnarvon died of nothing more sinister than an infected mosquito bite. Howard Carter, the leader of the expedition and the first man to enter the tomb, lived happily for many more years.

The poster for a 1955 movie which took a comic look at the idea of mummies coming back to life

The actor Christopher Lee in the 1959 film, "The Mummy"

Mummies in movies

The story of an angry mummy attacking the explorers who disturb it has been used in lots of movies. The first was made in 1932, not long after Tutankhamun's tomb was opened. People were intrigued by the spooky idea of a living mummy, and many more movies have followed.

Pyramid myths

The pyramids have thrown up just as many bizarre ideas as mummies have. Over the years, people have suggested that pyramids had the power to mummify dead cats left inside them, to preserve food and even to sharpen razor blades. People have also claimed that the Great Pyramid at Giza was built not by the ancient Egyptians but by aliens.

Fakes and frauds......................................

Mummies are big business, and are sold for huge sums of money. This has been true for centuries, and there have always been people who profited by making fake mummies.

Ancient frauds

A dishonest mummy-maker took a bird's head and made a fake body to go with it.

★ The "mummy" was carefully wrapped with bandages, and looked completely convincing.

Even genuinely ancient mummies aren't always quite what they seem. Animals were important in Egyptian religion, and millions of bird mummies were sold. But when birds were in short supply, some mummy-makers only put part of a bird inside each mummy. The rest was stuffed with rags, feathers and shards of pottery. This became so common that the government eventually had to ban it.

Mummy medicine

In the Middle Ages, a different sort of mummy trade began. Many people believed that powder made by grinding up mummies could cure all kinds of illnesses. For hundreds of years, people swallowed the disgusting stuff to help with sore throats, headaches and even broken bones.

There was a huge demand for the powder, and thousands of mummies were needed to make it all. Some merchants are said to have cashed in by murdering people, drying them in the sand and selling the bodies.

Mummy powder was a highly respected medicine. King Francis I of France used to sprinkle a little of it in his wine every day to keep himself healthy.

A container that was used to hold mummy powder

Internet links

For a link to a Web site where you can compare genuine ancient Egyptian objects with modern fakes, go to
www.usborne-quicklinks.com

Fact: Powdered mummy has even been used to make a type of paint, known as "mummy brown".

Murder mystery

In 2000, a seemingly incredible discovery was made in Pakistan. A perfectly preserved mummy was found, and it appeared to be the body of a Persian princess. It was said to be over 2,500 years old, and made by Egyptian experts. It looked like one of the most amazing finds ever made.

But the truth was far darker. Experts soon realized that the mummy was actually a fake made less than two years earlier. Even worse, the mummified woman may have been murdered to provide the body.

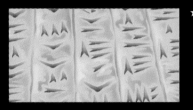 ★

Ancient writing on the mummy's coffin contained mistakes, which made experts suspicious.

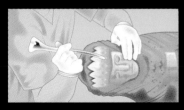

When experts examined the body, they discovered that the mummy was a modern fake.

The fake "Persian princess" mummy

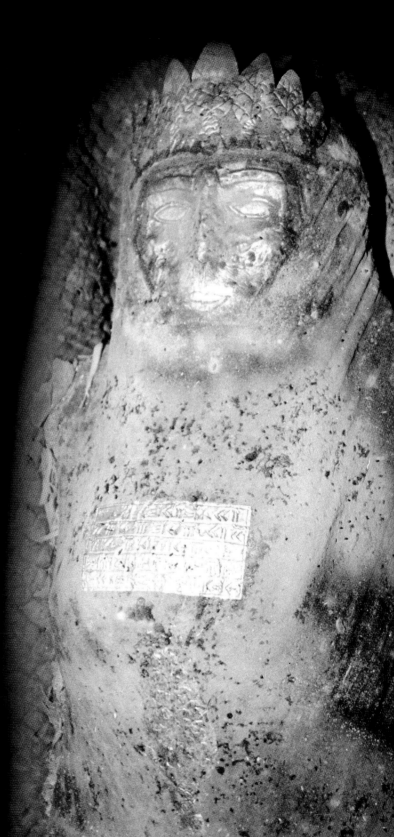

Unwrapping a mummy......

Once, the most common way of examining a mummy was simply to rip the bandages off. But this destroys a lot of evidence, and means the mummy can never be admired whole again. Today, scientists have a range of ways of studying a mummy without harming it.

Scanning the body

Machines used by doctors to look inside people are useful for examining mummies too. X-ray photographs can show us the inside of a mummy's body, as well as any amulets or jewels wrapped with it.

CAT (Computerized Axial Tomography) scanning is even more revealing. A CAT machine makes hundreds of pictures of a mummy's insides. These pictures are combined to form lifelike three-dimensional images which can be rotated.

On this X-ray you can see the outline of a coffin, and the skeleton of the mummy inside it.

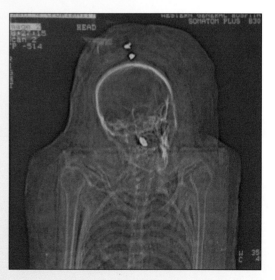

CAT scans of this unwrapped mummy head showed that the empty skull had been stuffed with linen to keep it in shape.

 Fact: X-rays of the pharaoh Ramesses II revealed that his big nose was stuffed with peppercorns to keep it in shape.

A delicate operation

When experts unwrap a mummy today, they do it extremely carefully. A large team of scientists works together, to find out as much as possible. Cloth experts study the bandages, while others look for preserved insects or seeds. Dentists inspect the teeth, which can tell them what kind of diet the person had.

A scientist examining a mummy's foot

Seeing inside

Experts also use a tool called an endoscope to study mummies without damaging them too much. This is a long, very narrow and flexible tube that can be inserted into a body through an opening, such as the nose. The endoscope takes pictures of the mummy's insides, and it can also remove tiny pieces of the body so that these can be studied.

An endoscope can even be inserted through a small hole in a coffin, so that the mummy can be examined without destroying the coffin.

Internet links

For a link to a Web site where you can see how X-rays and CAT scans helped to reveal the hidden secrets of a mummy, go to **www.usborne-quicklinks.com**

Thanks to an endoscope, scientists can view the mummy in this coffin on the TV screen.

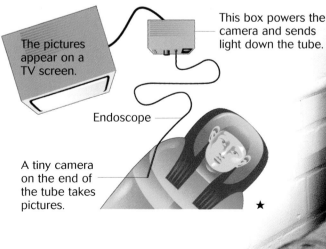

The pictures appear on a TV screen.

This box powers the camera and sends light down the tube.

Endoscope

A tiny camera on the end of the tube takes pictures.

★

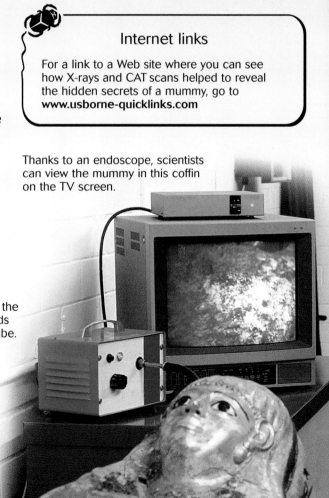

The mummy speaks

As well as looking inside mummies, experts use a variety of ingenious techniques to find out more about them. Preserved bodies can reveal a surprising number of facts about the distant past.

Internet links

For a link to a Web site where you can watch a mummy's face being gradually reconstructed with the help of computer graphics, go to **www.usborne-quicklinks.com**

Meet the relatives

Even tiny fragments of mummies can uncover secrets from thousands of years ago. One way to find out about a mummy is to analyze a chemical called DNA which is found in all living things, and also in things that were once alive.

People who are related to each other have similar DNA, so scientists can use it to trace the family relationships between mummies buried in different tombs.

A model showing the structure of DNA

The remains of a 4,000-year-old linen dress

Ancient styles

Sometimes, fragments of ancient cloth or even complete items of clothing are found in tombs. These show us what people wore, and how ancient clothes were made.

Face to face

Although mummies' faces were supposed to be perfectly preserved, only a few of them are. But we can still get a good idea of how they once looked. Using a model of a mummy's skull, a sculptor can reconstruct its face.

First, pegs are used to mark the thickness of the flesh. Then, layers of clay are added, and the shape of the face is built up from the skull. Some mummies were buried with a portrait of the dead person, so by recreating the face we can see how accurate these portraits were.

This model shows two different stages in reconstructing a mummy's face.

Pegs to mark the thickness of muscle and skin

Here you can see an ancient mummy portrait, and a finished model of the same woman.

Medical secrets

Studying mummies can also help us to learn what illnesses Egyptians suffered from, what sort of medical care they received, and even whether they had a bad back. All this helps experts to build up a detailed picture of life in ancient times.

Mummies around the world.............

The Egyptians are the most famous mummy-makers, but many other ancient peoples also preserved their dead. Here are just a few of them.

South America

China

This map shows the areas of the world where the mummies on these pages were found.

The oldest mummies

Lots of mummies have been found in the mountains and deserts of South America. The Chinchorro people from Chile were making mummies 7,000 years ago. This is 2,000 years before the Egyptians began making theirs.

The Chinchorro had their own way of making mummies. They took the body apart, and replaced the internal organs with clay and feathers. Then, they fastened the body back together with sticks and painted the mummy black.

The head of each Chinchorro mummy was covered with a clay mask.

Internet links

For a link to a Web site where you can read about mummies found around the world then play an online game and make a mummy, go to **www.usborne-quicklinks.com**

Inca mummies

The South American Inca people, who lived in Peru from around 3,000 years ago, made their dead kings into mummies. The kings were dressed in magnificent clothes and paraded through the streets at festivals.

Beautiful failures

In ancient China, people thought that a precious stone called jade had the power to preserve bodies. A few emperors, princes and nobles were buried inside suits made entirely from pieces of jade, sewn together with gold thread.

The only problem was that jade actually had no special powers at all. Although the amazing suits have survived to this day, the bodies of rulers inside them withered away thousands of years ago.

Here you can see a Chinese burial suit made from more than 2,000 pieces of jade.

Fact: The Chinese jade suits were so beautifully made that it took a team of skilled workers about 10 years to make each one.

Natural mummies

Lots of mummies are manmade but they can also be formed naturally, when bodies are preserved beneath sand, ice or boggy ground. Natural mummies have been found all over the world, from the ice fields of the Arctic to the baking deserts of Africa.

Bog bodies

Amazingly well preserved mummies can be formed when bodies are left in thick peat bogs. Several mummies found in the bogs of Denmark seem to have been killed as a sacrifice to the gods, then thrown into the bog.

This is Tollund Man, who was left in a bog in Denmark about 2,000 years ago. He had been hanged, and was found with the noose still around his neck.

Internet links

For a link to a Web site where you can find out more about the fascinating story of Ötzi the iceman and see photographs of his weapons, go to www.usborne-quicklinks.com

Desert mummies

Many mummies have been created by hot, dry desert sands. In Egypt and South America, bodies buried beneath the sand have been dried out and preserved.

One of the best known desert mummies is an Egyptian man who has been nicknamed Ginger. His ginger hair has survived along with his body for more than 5,000 years.

Ginger was buried along with a selection of pots, so that he would have somewhere to store food and drink in the next life.

Beneath the ice

Mummies are also formed when bodies are frozen by ice. The most famous ice mummy was discovered in 1991 by tourists wandering the Alps. It was a man who had died in the mountains over 5,000 years ago.

At first, no one was sure what killed the iceman. Some experts thought he had simply frozen to death in the mountains. But in 2001, experts studied him again and found an arrowhead buried in his shoulder. It now looks as though he was murdered.

Here you can see the iceman, nicknamed Ötzi, soon after he was discovered.

Fact: Many natural mummies still have traces of their last meal in their stomach, which helps to show what ancient people ate.

Unsolved mysteries

Mummies have taught us a massive amount about the ancient world. But some mummies create almost as many questions as they answer, and many secrets remain to be unravelled.

Gruesome ends

In 1975, experts at Manchester University in England examined the mummy of a 14-year-old Egyptian girl. To their surprise, they found that the lower parts of the mummy's legs were missing. No one is sure what lies behind this grisly mystery, but one theory is that the girl had been attacked by a crocodile.

The Manchester mummy was wrapped up to look unharmed. Here you can see its shoes.

Recycled treasures?

A local worker near the entrance of Tutankhamun's tomb soon after it was found

The boy pharaoh Tutankhamun died unexpectedly, but he was buried with amazing treasures. People have always been surprised that so many grave goods could have been made in such a short time. Some experts think that objects were removed from other tombs and reused. So the treasures may not be quite what they seem.

Was this beautiful statuette really made for Tutankhamun?

Tomb 55

In 1907, a new tomb was discovered in the Valley of the Kings. A splendid golden coffin contained a mummy - but whose? Unfortunately, the mummy was handled so roughly by the people who found it that it was reduced to bones.

Panels from a shrine in the tomb were decorated with the name of Queen Tiy, mother of the pharaoh Akhenaten. So the investigators decided the mummy must be hers. However, closer inspection of the bones showed that the mummy was a man - but which man?

This is the coffin found in tomb 55. Rather than helping to clear up the mystery, the coffin only created more questions.

Mystery man

Many experts think that the coffin in tomb 55 was originally made for Kiya, one of Akhenaten's wives. But it seems to have been altered to make the decorations suitable for a pharaoh. Could it be that the bones belong to the legendary Akhenaten himself? We may never know.

A statue of the pharaoh Akhenaten, a strange ruler who tried to change Egypt's religion

Internet links

For a link to a Web site where you can see photographs and plans of the mysterious tomb 55 and read more about it, go to
www.usborne-quicklinks.com

An ongoing quest......

Mummies, pyramids and other tombs have helped us to build up a fascinating picture of ancient Egypt. But our picture is far from complete, and new discoveries are made all the time.

The biggest tomb

In 1987, archaeologists in the Valley of the Kings found the entrance to a tomb. This tomb had been discovered before, but ancient floods had filled it with rubble and people thought it was unimportant.

However, the archaeologists now found that the tomb was far bigger than people had realized. Known as KV5, it is where the sons of the pharaoh Ramesses II were buried. It contains over a hundred chambers, and is the largest rock-cut tomb ever found in Egypt.

Some of the many bodies at the Valley of the Golden Mummies

Valley of the Golden Mummies

In 1993, archaeologists in Egypt made an amazing discovery, when a donkey accidentally stuck its leg through the roof of a chamber. Beneath the sand was a huge cemetery with as many as 10,000 mummies, some of them wearing beautiful masks covered in gold leaf. It will take years to examine all of the mummies, and they may shed new light on ancient Egypt.

Archaeologists examining remains at the Valley of the Golden Mummies

The tomb of Nefertiti

One of the most famous figures in Egyptian history is Queen Nefertiti, wife of the pharaoh Akhenaten. Nefertiti was legendary for her beauty, and has always fascinated historians. But we don't know where she was buried. Teams of archaeologists still dream of finding her final resting place, and discovering the truth behind the legend.

This famous carved head shows Queen Nefertiti. Finding her mummy might help to show whether she really looked like this.

Internet links

For a link to a Web site where you can explore the chambers inside KV5 and find out the latest news from the tomb, go to **www.usborne-quicklinks.com**

Reconstructing pyramids

Many unfinished pyramids and smaller pyramids built for Egyptian queens have been gradually destroyed over the centuries. But experts are now uncovering the remains, and using computer images to show how these magnificent buildings used to look.

A reconstruction showing the ruined pyramids of the queens of the pharaoh Pepy I as they once looked

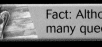 Fact: Although we have found the tombs of most Egyptian pharaohs, many queens and other royals remain to be discovered.

Using the Internet.............................

Most of the Web sites listed in this book can be accessed with a standard home computer and a Web browser (the software that enables you to display information from the Internet). We recommend:

- A PC with Microsoft® Windows® 98 or later version, or a Macintosh computer with System 9.0 or later, and 64Mb RAM
- A browser such as Microsoft® Internet Explorer 5, or Netscape® Navigator 4.7, or later versions
- Connection to the Internet via a modem (preferably 56Kbps) or a faster digital or cable line
- An account with an Internet Service Provider (ISP)
- A sound card to hear sound files

Extras

Some Web sites need additional programs, called plug-ins, to play sounds, or to show videos, animations or 3-D images. If you go to a site and you do not have the necessary plug-in, a message saying so will come up on the screen. There is usually a button on the site that you can click on to download the plug-in. Alternatively, go to **www.usborne-quicklinks.com** and click on **Net Help**. There you can find links to download plug-ins. Here is a list of plug-ins you might need:

RealPlayer® – lets you play videos and hear sound files.
QuickTime – enables you to view video clips.
Shockwave® – lets you play animations and interactive programs.
Flash™ – lets you play animations.

Help

For general help and advice on using the Internet, go to **Usborne Quicklinks** at **www.usborne-quicklinks.com** and click on **Net Help**. To find out more about how to use your Web browser, click on **Help** at the top of the browser, and then choose **Contents and Index**. You'll find a huge searchable dictionary containing tips on how to find your way around the Internet easily.

Internet safety

Remember to follow the Internet safety guidelines at the front of this book. For more safety information, go to **Usborne Quicklinks** and click on **Net Help**.

Computer viruses

A computer virus is a program that can seriously damage your computer. A virus can get into your computer when you download programs from the Internet, or in an attachment (an extra file) that arrives with an e-mail. We strongly recommend that you buy anti-virus software to protect your computer and that you update the software regularly.

Internet links

For links to Web sites where you can find out more about computer viruses, go to **www.usborne-quicklinks.com** and click on Net Help.

Macintosh and QuickTime are trademarks of Apple Computer, Inc., registered in the U.S. and other countries.
RealPlayer is a trademark of RealNetworks, Inc., registered in the U.S. and other countries.
Flash and Shockwave are trademarks of Macromedia, Inc., registered in the U.S. and other countries.

Index

Acknowledgements.......................

Every effort has been made to trace the copyright holders of the material in this book. If any rights have been omitted, the publishers offer to rectify this in any subsequent editions following notification. The publishers are grateful to the following organizations and individuals for their permission to reproduce material (t=top, m=middle, b=bottom, l=left, r=right):

Cover © Getty Images/Derek P. Redfearn; **p1** © Pictor International; **p2** © Sandro Vannini/CORBIS; **p3** ©Copyright The British Museum; **p4bl** ©Copyright The British Museum; **p4-5b** © Getty Images/Stephen Studd; **p5r** © Gianni Dagli Orti/CORBIS; **p6l** © Roger Wood/CORBIS; **p7** ©Copyright The British Museum; **p8tl** ©Copyright The British Museum; **p8-9b** © Kenneth Garrett/National Geographic Image Collection; **p9** ©Copyright The British Museum; **p10** ©Copyright The British Museum; **p11l, r** ©Copyright The British Museum; **p12bl** ©Copyright The British Museum; **p13** (l) © Gianni Dagli Orti/CORBIS, (r) ©Copyright The British Museum; **p14** (l) © Royalty-Free/CORBIS, (r) © Archivo Iconografico, S.A./CORBIS; **p15** © Roger Wood/CORBIS; **p16** © Andrew Bayuk; **p18-19b** © Getty Images/David Sutherland; **p19r** ©Copyright The British Museum; **p20** © Gianni Dagli Orti/CORBIS; **p21** (tr) ©Copyright The British Museum, (b) © Getty Images/PhotoLink; **p22** (l) © University College Museum, London, UK/Bridgeman Art Library, (r) © Bettmann/CORBIS; **p23** (t) © Getty Images/Hisham F. Ibrahim, (b) © ART on FILE/CORBIS; **p24** © Roger Wood/CORBIS; **p25** (tl) © Hulton-Deutsch Collection/CORBIS, (b) © AAA Collection Ltd.; **p26** (tr) © Griffith Institute, Oxford, (bl) © Robert Partridge: The Ancient Egypt Picture Library; **p27** (l) © Camera Press, (r) © TRIP/J Pilkington; **p28** (bl, br) ©Copyright The British Museum, (tr) © Gian Berto Vanni/CORBIS; **p28-29t** © Sandro Vannini/CORBIS; **p29r** ©Copyright The British Museum; **p30** (l) © Stapleton Collection/CORBIS, (r) © Robert Partridge: The Ancient Egypt Picture Library; **p31** (l) © CinemaPhoto/Corbis, (r) © Hammer/Kobal Collection; **p32** © Science Museum/Science and Society Picture Library; **p33** © Reuters; **p34** (l) ©Copyright The British Museum, (r) © Trustees of the National Museums of Scotland ; **p35** (t) © Peter Menzel/Science Photo Library, (br) © The Manchester Museum; **p36** (r) © Petrie Museum of Egyptian Archaeology, UCL.28614B; **p37** (tr) © Department of Archaeology, Bristol Museums and Art Gallery, (bl) ©Copyright The British Museum, (br) © University of Manchester (Fatima Head kept at the British Museum); **p38** © Chris Sharp/South American Pictures; **p39** © Robert Harding Picture Library/Alamy; **p40** © Chris Lisle/CORBIS; **p40-41b** © Viennareport/Camera Press; **p41t** ©Copyright The British Museum; **p42** (bl) © The Manchester Museum, (tr) © Getty Images/General Photographic Agency; **p43** (r) © Archivo Iconografico/CORBIS; **p44** © Sandro Vannini/CORBIS **p44-45t** © Ron Watts/CORBIS; **p45** (br) © Mediatheque EDF/Silicon Worlds.

Photographic manipulation by John Russell.